CROAGH PATRICK

IRELAND'S HOLY MOUNTAIN

EDITED BY HARRY HUGHES

Acknowledgements

This book would not have been possible without the assistance of many people and we extend our gratitude to them. All the amateur and professional photographers, who entered both competitions in 2002 and 2003. The judges of the 2002 competition, Mr. Michael Gibbons and Mr. Tom Byrne, and the judges of the 2003 competition, Mr. Liam Lyons and Mr. Des Clinton. Our thanks to the staff of Westport Library and Mayo County Library for allowing the exhibitions in Westport Library, and to Mr. Liam Lyons for officiating in 2003 and Mr. Sean Staunton in 2004. The graphic artists who designed this book, Mr. Alan Dowling and Mr. Paul Malone. Thanks also to Mr. Michael Gibbons and Mr. Gerry Walsh for the chapter on archaeology. Special thanks to Elisabeth Farrell for proof reading. Our gratitude to the members of the Croagh Patrick Archaeological Committee: Very Rev. Denis Carney, Harry Hughes, Owen Campbell, Paddy Foy, John Groden, Cathal Hughes, Gerry Walsh, Sean Staunton, Michael Gibbons, Leo Morahan, Breda Hyland.
Patrons: Most Rev. Dr. Michael Neary, Archbishop of Tuam and Most Rev. Dr. Joseph Cassidy, retired Archbishop of Tuam.

Centenary Celebrations - St. Patrick's Oratory 1905 – 2005
This book celebrates the centenary of St. Patrick's Oratory on the summit of Croagh Patrick. The following was the schedule of events organised to celebrate the centenary in Westport Parish from Garland Friday to Reek Sunday 2005:

29th July - Garland Friday – Mass in St. Patrick's Oratory on the summit of Croagh Patrick at 10am.

29th July - Friday evening – Open air Mass in Murrisk at 7.30pm, followed by a tree planting ceremony by Fr. Denis Carney, Administrator of Westport Parish.

30th July - Saturday evening – Mass in St. Mary's Church, Westport. Celebrated by Dr. Michael Neary, Archbishop of Tuam. Centenary book launch by Dr. Michael Neary in the Croagh Patrick Information Centre at 8.30pm. – Book title *Croagh Patrick – Ireland's Holy Mountain*

31st July - Reek Sunday – Mass celebrated by Dr. Michael Neary in St. Patrick's Oratory on the summit of Croagh Patrick at 10.30am. After Mass Dr. Neary will unveil the centenary plaque, which is positioned over the door of St. Patrick's Oratory. Mass will be celebrated every half an hour from 8am to 2pm.

St. Patrick's Oratory
It is planned to open St. Patrick's Oratory on Croagh Patrick each day from 11.30am to 4pm during July and August this centenary year. A guide will be available to provide information or assistance and pilgrims can sign a visitor's book.

St. Patrick's Black Bell
St. Patrick's Black Bell is the centrepiece of an exhibition - *Religion and Magic, Creideamh agus Draíocht* - at the National Museum of Country Life, Turlough Park, Castlebar, from May to October 2005.

First published in 2005 by the Croagh Patrick Archaeological Commitee.

British Library cataloguing in Publication Data
ISBN 0-9536086-4-6

St. Patrick's Oratory *By Harry Hughes*

Contents

Preface

Dr Michael Neary
Archbishop of Tuam

Croagh Patrick is flamboyant and colourful as some warm-hearted faithed corner of Christendom, wrote the poet Patrick Kavanagh in 1940. There have been many challenges to this nation's deep spirituality and religious faith since Kavanagh, the poetic voice of the Irish countryside, wrote these evocative lines over sixty years ago. At the time, our Christian and Catholic faith seemed indomitable. It seems fair to say that much has changed since.

The continued popularity of pilgrimage to Croagh Patrick, however, indicates a still persistent and perhaps ineradicable instinct towards the transcendent on our parts. This deeply spiritual mountain, with its dramatic contours, continues to provide a beacon of hope for the many whose faith has been diminished by the rise of materialism and the omnipresent challenges of consumerism. The traditional details of its pilgrimage perfectly juxtapose the notions of suffering and redemption. The social dimension of the experience, particularly on Reek Sunday, disputes the pervasiveness of individualism and celebrates the notions of communality and belonging as an intrinsic part of our various spiritual journeys.

The publication of this photographic book in the year that celebrates the centenary of the building of St. Patrick's Oratory is a wonderful testament to the continuance of religious faith at its most basic and simple. The photographers are both witnesses and participants in a cross-millennial religious ritual that links St. Patrick, our patron saint, with contemporary society. The significance of St. Patrick's message is brought once again into central focus as it subtly and beautifully reverberates through these varied images.

We must acknowledge and give thanks for the work of Dr. John Healy, late Archbishop of Tuam, and Canon Michael McDonald, for their foresight in building this oratory which for a century has provided that symbolic shelter and sanctuary that is an intrinsic part of our Church's message and belief. We also pray and give thanks for the builders of St. Patrick's Oratory, and the many priests and stewards who organise the pilgrimage on the last Sunday of July each year. We gratefully pray for all those associated with organising devotion on Croagh Patrick since 1905, many of whose names are not recorded but whose legacy lives on. Through the pages of this book, let us celebrate with the people of Westport parish the unique gift of Croagh Patrick and heartily pray that all those who come on pilgrimage to its slopes will find contentment, renewal and peace in their lives.

Finally, I wish to thank all those who entered the photographic competitions and I warmly compliment the work of the Croagh Patrick Archaeological Committee and its chairman Mr. Harry Hughes.

Michael Neary,
Archbishop of Tuam.

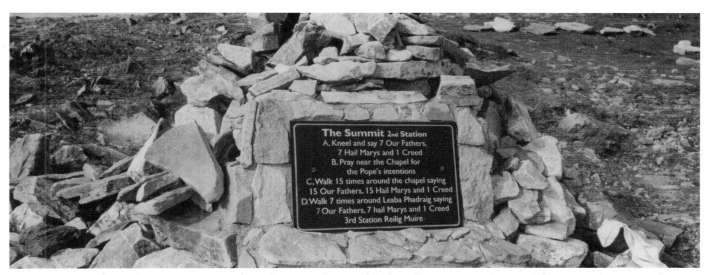

Pilgrims Penance *By Sean J. Hoban*

Foreword

Harry Hughes
Chairman, Croagh Patrick Archaeological Committee

The small church situated at the peak of Ireland's pyramidal holy mountain, Croagh Patrick, is a moving and poignant symbol of Ireland's faith. The fact that it was built near the site of an Early Christian oratory (circa 430-890 AD) deepens its historic significance and weaves a colourful thread into the ancient recesses and roots of our heritage.

Dwarfed by the dramatic presence of a mountain, whose amazing story predates Christian worship, the oratory stands as a testament to a fragile humanity's elevation through the rich rituals of formal religious worship.

In 1905, the Archbishop of Tuam, Dr. John Healy, and Canon Michael McDonald organised the building of St. Patrick's Oratory. Having raised £100 through donations from pilgrims and emigrants, they employed architect William H. Byrne and building contractor Walter Heneghan. The oratory was built over a six month period, by twelve local men. The materials were drawn up the mountain by donkey and horse.

While Ireland has undergone a series of revolutionary changes since the building of the oratory a century ago, the ancient tradition and practise of pilgrimage to Croagh Patrick continues to be widely observed. The annual Reek Sunday pilgrimage attracts people from all over the world.

In 2002 and 2003 the Croagh Patrick Archaeological Committee held photographic competitions which attracted a large number of participants. Many of these images now, in a new context, mark the centenary of the oratory through the pages of this book. The medium of photography uniquely freeze-frames a moment in time; it can capture the nuance of a fleeting expression or focus on the spontaneity of a gesture. While miniaturising the panoramic, the camera can still reach into the minutiae of nature's endless visual gifts.

The collection of photography in this book endeavours to chronicle the generations of people who have interacted with this dramatically spiritual place. The natural amphitheatre of Clew Bay provides an ideal setting for these individual studies and portraits.

While the holy mountain has stood witness to thousands of years of Neolithic, Celtic and Christian culture, its tiny oratory, too, has withstood the gales and storms of a tumultuous century in world history. Who knows what the future will bring. There is some certainty, however, that pilgrimage to this holy place will continue to invigorate the human spirit and hold sacrosanct our many traditions.

Despite the failure of our heritage agencies to properly address Croagh Patrick's significance as a national monument, its national and international importance continues to be salvaged by local communities. It should never be forgotten that it was through their convictions that the threat of mining on the mountain was averted in the 1980s.

I wish to thank the Murrisk Development Association and the members of the Croagh Patrick Archaeological Committee for their continued support since 1994.

Harry Hughes
Chairman, Croagh Patrick Archaeological Committee

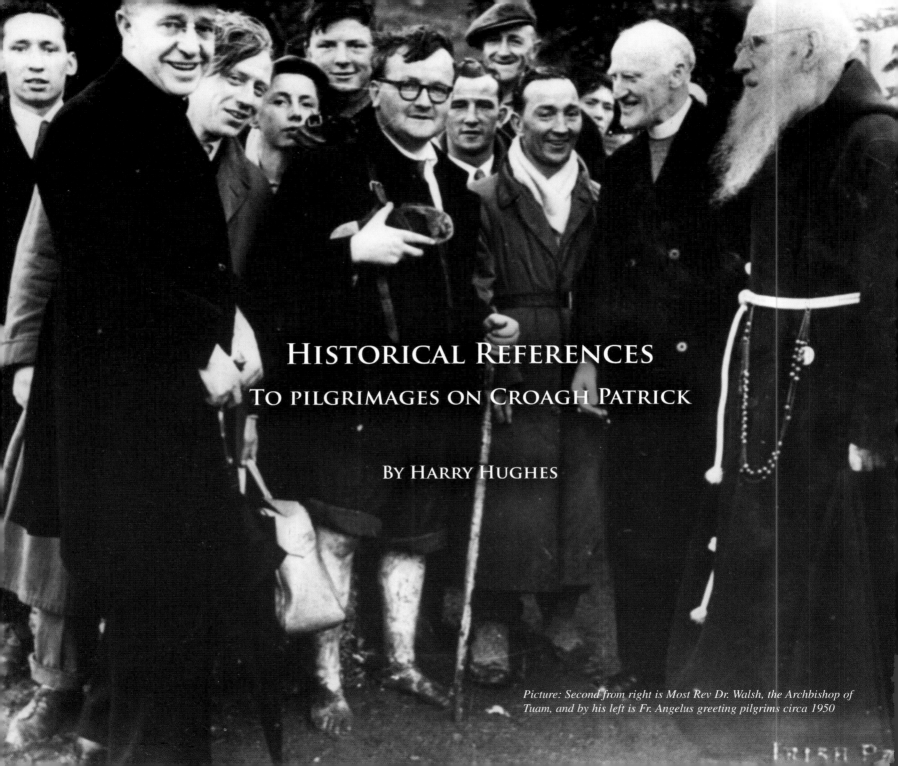

HISTORICAL REFERENCES

TO PILGRIMAGES ON CROAGH PATRICK

BY HARRY HUGHES

Picture: Second from right is Most Rev Dr. Walsh, the Archbishop of Tuam, and by his left is Fr. Angelus greeting pilgrims circa 1950

Historical References to Pilgrimages on Croagh Patrick

By Harry Hughes

The Book of Armagh tells us that St. Patrick prayed and fasted on the mountain in the 5th century AD. There are numerous historical references to pilgrimages on Croagh Patrick and these illustrate the wonderful heritage and legacy of St. Patrick.

824 – The Archbishop of Armagh had an episcopal dispute with the Archbishop of Tuam, as Armagh claimed dues from Teampall Phádraig. This shows the church was being used.

1079 – From the *Annals of the Four Masters* we learn that Torlach O'Brien invaded Connacht from the sea with a great army and expelled Ruaidhrí O Connor from the kingdom of Connacht and plundered the Cruach (the Reek).

1113 – The *Annals of Ulster* record that 'A ball of fire [lightning] came on the night of the feast of Patrick [17 March] on Cruachain Aighle and destroyed thirty of those fasting.' This clearly shows the existence of a pilgrimage, a night vigil and penitential exercises being performed.

1152 – The historical memoirs of the O'Connors of Connacht reveal that Tiernan O'Rourke, chief of Briefney, was absent on pilgrimage to Croagh Patrick in 1152 when his wife eloped with Dermot Mac Murrough, King of Leinster.

1185 – Jocelyn, a Cistercian monk from Scotland, wrote a Life of Saint Patrick and he tells us 'That many are accustomed to spend the night awake and fasting on the mount.'

1224 – *The Annuals of Loch Cé* state that the only crime committed in Connacht was a robbery on the way to the Reek. The robber was punished by having his hands and feet cut off.

1432 – Pope Eugene IV granted an indulgence to the penitents on Croagh Patrick. From this indulgence and other previous references, it can be assumed that the pilgrimage was the charge of the monks of Aghagower and that the popularity of the pilgrimage led to an episcopal dispute about the revenues and the routes to the Reek being subject to robbery.

1457 – Pope Callistus III wrote a letter granting 'permission to Hugh O'Malley, Augustinian friar of the house of Corpus Christi, to establish a church and friary in the half quarter of Murrisk.' The Murrisk friars seem to have taken over the organising of the pilgrimage from the Aghagower monastery.

1485 – In the Vatican archives there is a letter written by Octavian, Archbishop of Armagh, to two priests from Lyon (France) to testify that they had visited the devout pilgrimage on the Holy mountain, on which St. Patrick had fasted 40 days and nights.

1652 – Fr. James O'Mahony wrote that: ' On this mountain of Holy Patrick is held the most widely celebrated pilgrimage of the whole Kingdom, one begun and established by Saint Patrick himself.' From the sixteenth century the Irish church was facing prosecution from the state-imposed religion. This led to many monasteries and abbeys being abandoned, but 'Turas na Cruiche' provided a means of protecting the faith without liturgical services. The procurator of the ecclesiastical province of Tuam in 1661 directs 'that the plenary indulgence anciently granted to the pilgrims at the holy places of Aran and Croagh Patrick should be continued and renewed.'

1798 – De Latocayne states: 'Croagh Patrick is a very celebrated place for the penitences of the faithful.' The pilgrimage started very soon after St. Patrick's visit in 441 AD and the practice of imitating the Saints penitential exercise has survived 1500 years.

Pilgrims visiting Westport

Cruachán Aigli

Long before Saint Patrick's visit, the Reek was known as Cruachán Aigil. The origin of the name Cruachán Aigli is set down in the 'Dindsenchas,' a legendary account of Irish place-names translated by Professor Gwynn.

'Aigli son of Derg (Red his face);
Him Cromderg son of Connra slew:
From that deed of savage force the name
Aigle is given to Garbos.
Cruachan Garbois the learned of this Land
used to call it:
Thenceforth its name is Cruachán Aigle, till
The day of judgement.'

Tíreachán writing in Latin circa 670 in the *Book of Armagh* relates Saint Patrick's visit to the Reek. Tíreachán, a native of Connacht, spoke in the vernacular (i.e. Irish), but he wrote in Latin as it was the language of the Roman Church. Tíreachán wrote 'Ad Montem Egli' and two sentences later wrote 'Crochan Aigli.' This shows he uses the native name of the Reek and he translates this name also into Latin as 'Montem Aigli'. He refers to Murrisk as 'Muiresc Aigli', which shows the area was known as Aigli and the mountain as Crochan Aigli.

Westport Quay and Croagh Patrick

Muiresc' means 'Sea Swamp' and 'Cruach' means conical mountain, or stacked up hill or Reek. Colgan in his translation of the *Tripartite Life of Saint Patrick* (1647) noted that Cruachán Aigli means Mons Aquilae or Mount Eagle, but this leaves unexplained why Tíreachán did not translate 'Crochan Aigli' into Mons Aquilae. Colgan's belief that Aigli was a reflex of Aquila apparently had no basis in fact. It was no doubt based on his awareness of the existence of the words 'Aicil', 'Acail' (eagle) in Irish, this being simply an Irish transformation of the Latin word aquila, and such explanations, based on some apparent similarity between words, are not an uncommon source of confusion.

Colgan's English translation received widespread coverage. In 1768 John Browne, a local landlord, received the title Baron Mount Eagle, and in 1771 became the first Earl of Altamont. The coat of arms for Westport town incorporates an eagle. John O'Donovan in 1838 states: 'It is curious that a part of the ridge extending eastwards from the peak or Reek is still called Mount Eagle.'

The name Cruach Phádraig started to gain prominence over Cruachán Aigli from the tenth to the thirteenth century. In the sixteenth century when many Irish place-names were given an anglicised version, Cruach Phádraig became widely known as Croagh Patrick. One of the first recorded versions is in Browne's map of Mayo in 1585.

Pilgrims Ascending Croaghpatrick.

Pilgrims path before St. Patrick's statue was erected in 1928

chapel

Church Buildings

The second traditional station on the Reek before the new church was built in 1905 included a visit to the old church. John O'Donovan states in 1838: 'He [the pilgrim] enters the little chapel called *Teampall Phádraig*… the pilgrim kneels at the altar and repeats his prayers'. St. Patrick while on the mountain would have said mass and tradition has it that he built a rude little chapel, later known as Teampall Phádraig.

More than three hundred years after St. Patrick had been on the mountain, we find reference to his little chapel as still existing on the summit. The Archbishop of Armagh was entitled to exact annual revenue from every church that had been founded by St. Patrick in any part of Ireland. In the course of time this primitive chapel fell into decay, and, as the Reek had continued to be a place of devotion, another was erected on its site. In the year 1216, Felix O'Ruane, Archbishop of Tuam, appealed to Rome against the claim of Armagh for a tax on this church. Pope Honorius III on 30th July 1216 decided that as this chapel had been erected by the Archbishop of Tuam, no tribute from it could be claimed by the Archbishop of Armagh. Pope Eugene IV granted an indulgence in 1432 to 'penitents who visit and give alms for the repair of the chapel of Saint Patrick'.

Downing states in 1680: 'On the hill called Croagh Patrick there is a chapel dedicated to St. Patrick upon the top thereof where many came from afar in the summer season.' *A Frenchman's Walk through Ireland,* written by M. De Latocnayne in 1797, mentions this same church.

In 1838 John O'Donovan gives a good description of the church: '…Teampall Phádraig which is sixteen feet long and eight broad to the east end, where the stone altar is placed and only five feet at the entrance. Its east gable is eight and a half feet high.' Ordnance Survey Maps of 1839 and 1920 show Temple Patrick close to Leaba Phádraig.

London Daily Chronicle, 1904, has an article entitled *An Irish Pilgrimage* – 'On the mountaintop he [St. Patrick] built a small chapel. The place may be seen, in a hollow like a little crater, close to the very summit. It had been roofed over lately with a few sheets of corrugated iron held down by a pile of rocks.'

All this evidence clearly shows that there was a primitive church from the earliest time to 1904 before the new church was built. Fortunately from a few photographs preserved over 100 years there is also photographic evidence of this church. Mass was last celebrated in it on 14 August 1904 by Very Rev. M. McDonald. The foundation of the 1500-year-old church still exists on the summit.

Pilgrims attending Mass in 1904

Stephens and Clarke Temporary Chapel

The pilgrimage was declining after very severe famine in the 1840s. Rev. John Stephens and Rev. Michael Clarke, conscious of the great revival of all matters Irish, set about restoring the Croagh Patrick pilgrimage to its former glory. They proceeded to rebuild the old church, which had no roof, as the following passage from *The Irish Builder* Magazine of February 1883 states: 'An elevated chapel – the following memo taken from a contemporary has been handed to us – "Westport Oct 6th, 1882 – at the hour of 4 a.m. this morning the Rev. John Stephens R.C.C. Athenry and the Rev. Michael Clarke, Dublin accompanied by two architects and a large number of workmen, left here for Croagh Patrick, bringing with them the necessary materials consisting of sheet iron and metal pillars etc. for erecting a temporary chapel on the summit of the mountain".'

On the last Friday of July 1883, Fr. Stephens, Fr. Clarke and Fr. Lawrence O'Brien celebrated Mass for 600 people. However, Rev. John Stephens's support for the Land League put him in disfavour with the civil authorities. He was also a critic of Archbishop MacEvilly which led to his dismissal from the Archdiocese in 1886. The action halted their planned revival of the ancient pilgrimage and it was not until the advent of a new Archbishop in 1903 that the revival actually happened. Very little is known or written about the temporary church from 1882 – 1905. However, photographs from the following pages show that Fr. M. McDonald celebrated the last mass in the temporary church on 14th August 1904. Afterwards the Archbishop of Tuam, Most Rev. Dr. Healy, stood on its roof to preach a sermon.

Stephens and Clarke Chapel. Pilgrimage on the 14th August 1904

Revival of Old Pilgrimage

Year 1903

Dr. John Healy became Archbishop of Tuam on 17th March 1903. Fr. Michael McDonald, Administrator in Westport, sought permission from Tuam to revive the celebration of Mass on the summit of Croagh Patrick. He could hardly have a better ally, as Dr. Healy had an intense interest in antiquarian subjects. He wrote *The Life and Writings of Saint Patrick*. Fr. McDonald having obtained permission set about with great zeal, organising Mass for 16th August 1903. Special trains were organised by the Midland Great Western Railway Company for pilgrims.

On the morning of 16th August, the weather was inclement. Fr. McDonald rode up the mountain on a pony and then ascended 'Casán Phádraig' by foot. Mass was celebrated in Fr. John Stephens's iron-clad church at noon by Fr. McDonald and afterwards he gave an eloquent sermon apologising for Dr. Healy's inability to attend and he quoted the Archbishop: 'He says that if this holy mountain of ours were situated in any other country in Europe it would be made a place of national pilgrimage for the people of the country and he is determined… to make this holy mountain, henceforth a place of national pilgrimage.' Many people spent the day performing the station of the Reek after Mass.

Year 1904

The organisation of the second national pilgrimage to Croagh Patrick fell to Fr. McDonald. A local committee arranged for special trains. The steam-packet companies plying between Westport, Sligo, and the Scottish and English ports brought many pilgrims. Several bands were booked to play sacred music.

On 14th August 1904, Dr. Healy, Archbishop of Tuam, and Dr. Lyster, Bishop of Achonry, climbed the Reek, but again the mountain gave no shelter from the weather. Fr. McDonald celebrated Mass at 12am in the little cavern-like church and afterwards Dr. Healy stood on its roof to give a short address to the pilgrims standing in the rain. 'Think of this mountain as the symbol of Ireland's enduring faith and of the constancy and success with which the Irish people faced the storms of persecution during many woeful centuries. It is therefore the fitting type of Irish faith and Ireland's nationhood which nothing has ever shaken and with God's blessing nothing can ever destroy.'

Dr. Lyster was reported in the *Mayo News* as saying: 'In all his travels he had never beheld a more affecting display of spontaneous and unrehearsed devotion.' Dr. Healy wrote to Fr. McDonald on 21st August 1904 and instructed him to erect a suitable church on top of the Reek.

Most Rev. Dr John Healy with Fr. Canavan to his right. (Note the reporters on Dr. Healy's left side.)

Year 1905

Details of the new church are given later in this book. Sunday, 30th July 1905, witnessed an historic occasion on Croagh Patrick, as Dr. Healy dedicated the newly-erected church of Saint Patrick. The now usual arrangements with the railway companies ensured a huge crowd, estimated at 10,000 pilgrims. Rev. McDonald celebrated the first sacrifice of the Mass at 12 pm on the altar presented by the Convent of Mercy, Westport and positioned at the front door with over 20 priests in attendance.

His Grace Dr. Healy then addressed the vast crowd from the front door of the new oratory and spoke about St. Patrick's vigil on Cruachán Aigli. He stated: 'They alone had always venerated the footsteps of St. Patrick and they alone practised the fasting and prayer of which he [St. Patrick] was himself so bright an example.' He concluded by thanking Fr. McDonald and Mr. Walter Heneghan the contractor on their great work. He also welcomed Dean Phelan, representing Most Rev. Dr. Thomas Carr, who had generously sent a subscription. Dean Phelan, the Dean of Melbourne, then addressed the crowd and expressed his joy at being there and explained the plight and the faith of the Irish exiles in Australia.

For the rest of the summer's day many hundreds performed the stations and viewed the interior of the church. The Westport brass band played a number of airs before the dedication ceremony, conducted by Mr. Peter McConville. A second pilgrimage was arranged for the 15th August (Feast of the Assumption) and Fr. Canavan celebrated Mass.

The first wedding on the Reek took place during 1907.
This photograph probably includes some of the wedding party.

Building an Elevated Church

Rev. Michael McDonald set about the erection of a new oratory immediately after the 1904 pilgrimage and employed William H. Byrne as architect and Mr. Walter Heneghan of Louisburg as building contractor. In a tent upon the windy summit lived Mr. Thomas Duffy, the carpenter, Mr. Charles O'Malley, the apprentice stone mason, Mr. Walter Heneghan the contractor and his fifteen year old son Patrick, who once a day took messages down the mountain.

During the early excavation of the site a skull and some bones were unearthed and the builders believed those to be of Robert Binn, a hermit who lived on Croagh Patrick in the 1830s. Patrick Heneghan recorded some years later that he was away but he believed that the priest was present when the bones were reburied at the east end of the church. The Ordnance Survey of 1839 shows Robert Binn's grave thirty metres east of the church, so it remains a mystery as to who was buried there.

The elements, in their various guises over six months, assaulted the men working on the chapel and Mr. O'Malley recalled that they were nearly lost one night in a terrible storm. A heavy plank fell across Walter Heneghan's legs and pinned him to the floor. Remarkably, however, there were three tourists on the summit, two of them from London, and all three were doctors. While they were not able to do much about the blue-black bruises, they could assure Mr. Heneghan that he had no broken bones.

All the materials used were local, and as much work as could be done at the bottom of the mountain, such as making the iron girders, doors, cutting timber and numbering it, was performed there. All the necessary materials, such as sand and cement, were drawn up the mountain on donkey or horse at a rate of five shillings per three hundredweight. Water was drawn from Garraí Mór (third station) to the summit.

Mr. Charles O'Malley, when climbing the mountain in 1961 at over eighty years of age, recalled that he carried the six iron girders on his shoulder up Cásan Phádraig, and when these were assembled they weighed three hundredweight each. Twelve local men were employed for the six months of the construction and their wages were a sovereign a week for a skilled man and half a crown for labourers, who daily trudged up and down the mountain. Patrick Heneghan said the wages were always paid in Campbell's public house at the foot of the Reek.

Crowd attending the dedication of the new oratory in 1905. Notice how the men are mainly to the left and women to the right. Some instruments from Peter MacConville's brass band are in the centre of the photograph. The brass band played again for pilgrims in Westport to celebrate the fiftieth anniversary of the church on the summit and Peter MacConville was the only member from the 1905 band still alive in 1955.

One of those who built the church was John Clarke of James's Street, Westport. He was a step-brother of Charles O'Malley and daily cycled the six miles to the foot of the mountain before commencing his ascent. Other people involved were Tim Philbin, Austin Ruddy, Mr. Brady, Mr. Joyce and Dan Gavin. No record has been kept of the others involved.

The total cost of the building was about one hundred pounds and this was mainly collected from emigrants and subsequent pilgrimages. (The cost was based on a time and material basis.) Mrs. Mary Maher, a good friend of Dr. Healy and an ardent believer in the Croagh Patrick pilgrimage, subscribed five pounds. Cardinal Moran, when Bishop of Ossory, also subscribed five pounds. The following words are inscribed on a tablet over the door:

*'A.M.D.G. / In Honorem S. Patricii /
Aedificandum Curaverunt / Johannes Healy,
Archiepiscopus Tuamensis / et / Michael
McDonald Adm. Westport / M.D.C.C.C.V. /
Architectur Guil H. Byrne Opifex Wualt
Heneghan.'*

One hundred years later on 31st July 2005, Most Rev. Dr. Michael Neary will unveil a plaque positioned over the door of St. Patrick's Oratory inscribed with the following:

*'This plaque was unveiled on Reek Sunday 2005,
by Most Rev. Dr. Michael Neary, Archbishop of Tuam,
to commemorate the centenary of the building of St. Patrick's Oratory
1905 - 2005'*

This 1905 photograph shows the old church in the foreground and the new church in the background.

Pilgrims arrival at Croaghpatrick Hotel.

Pilgrims arrival in Murrisk

Picture Right: **Croagh Patrick from Killadangan** *By Michael O'Sullivan*

Croagh Patrick, County Mayo

In the archaeology

and history of Ireland

By Michael Gibbons & Gerry Walsh

Croagh Patrick, Co. Mayo, in the Archaeology and History of Ireland

By Michael Gibbons and Gerry Walsh

Introduction

Croagh Patrick (c.2,510ft/765m) dominates the landscape of southwest Mayo, both physically and spiritually. Perhaps due to its distinctive pyramidal form it has been regarded as religiously significant since at least the sixth century AD. A church built on top of the mountain in 1905 is still in use today. The ridge of Croagh Patrick is bounded by Clew Bay to the north, by extensive tracks of blanket bog to the south and west and by low hills to the east. This well-defined upland area slopes dramatically into a narrow coastal strip, which contains rich agricultural and marine resources.

The mountain is home to one of the most extraordinary and ancient pilgrimages surviving in Western Europe. There are three pilgrimages annually to the mountain, the largest of which is that held on the last Sunday in July, the other two are held on *Aoine Chrom-Dubh* (the last Friday in July) and on the 15th of August (the Feast of the Assumption). Local people mainly frequent the two smaller pilgrimages. The main pilgrimage is, without doubt, one of Ireland's great cultural treasures and, in an increasingly secularised and sanitised world, its continued vitality constitutes a living link with both our ancient native spirituality and with a wider international custom of venerating the high places as links between the Heavens and the Earth.

Although named after our national saint, it seems, in earlier times, to have been referred to as *Cruacháin Aigli*. This was translated into Latin as *Mons Aigli*, which was later translated by Colgan (incorrectly) as "Mount Eagle." *Aigli* actually seems to be derived from an old name for the region, Murrisk being referred to as *Muiresc Aigli* in the same text. The mountain is also sometimes referred to as "the Cruach" in the written sources.

The summit of Croagh Patrick from the West, showing the outline of the hill-top rampart.

Patrick's *Confessions* does not refer to the mountain directly. It is mainly a narrative of his spiritual life and contains little that can be used as specific geographical information. Patrick's biographies began to be written over a century after his death and contain much mythological material related to the claims of various contemporary ecclesiastical powers. The earliest extant biography dates to the late 7th century and is preserved in the *Book of Armagh*. Tírechán, the author, relates that Patrick was instructed by God to go to the wood of *Focluth*, which is usually taken to be in North Mayo. Tírechán recounts that Patrick was greeted on the mountain by the souls of unborn saints who welcomed him. As the prominence of Patrick in both historiography and folk memory grew, his significance as a propaganda asset also increased. The spread of his cult was linked with the growth of Armagh as the dominant ecclesiastical centre on the island.

The tradition of Patrick's stay on the mountain developed over time. In the tenth century *Bethu Phátraic,* the Saint fasts on the summit for Lent. He is tormented by demonic birds, which he drives off with his bell, after which angelic white birds serenade him. While on the mountain he is reputed to have won a special boon from God, the right to judge the Irish on the Last Day. The tradition that Patrick banished snakes from Ireland dates from the 12th century and became attached to Croagh Patrick. It was said that the Saint had banished the serpents into either Clew Bay or the hollow known as *Log na nDeamhan* (the hollow of the devil) while on the mountain. Also in later examples of the tradition, Patrick defeats *Crom Dubh*, a reputed pre-Christian divinity/demon who Patrick is reputed to have challenged on high places elsewhere as well.

Archaeological excavation team on first day of dig.
Left to right: Michael Gibbons (Director of survey), Owen Campbell (Committee),
John Cummins, Gerry Walsh (Site Director) Michael John Ball and William Thornton.

The traditional date of Patrick's arrival in Ireland is 432 AD, putting the date of his supposed stay on Croagh Patrick at about 441 AD. This seems to be a later addition by the annalists trying to make sense of the historical record. This created an interpretative difficulty as Pope Celestine sent a Bishop named Palladius to "the Irish believing in Christ" in 431 AD, casting doubt on Patrick's claim to be a pioneer. Recent scholarship has restored Patrick's primacy as the earliest Christian missionary, placing him in Ireland earlier, possibly as early as 400 AD.

The earliest contemporary reference to *Teampall Phádraig*, the church on the summit, seems to date to 824 when it caused a dispute between the Archbishops of Tuam and Armagh. In 1079 Torlach O'Brien plundered the mountain during an expedition against Ruadhrí O'Connor and on 17th March 1113 lightning killed thirty pilgrims fasting on the summit. Jocelyn, a Cistercian monk from Scotland, who wrote a life of St. Patrick, mentioned the custom of spending the night fasting on the summit in the late twelfth century. In 1432 Pope Eugene IV granted an indulgence to penitents on Croagh Patrick and after 1457 the pilgrimage seems to have come under the control of the Augustinian Friars who were granted permission to establish a Friary at Murrisk that stands to this day.

The Catholic Church came under sustained attack in the centuries after the Reformation but the tradition of pilgrimage continued and is mentioned in 1652 and again in 1798. A church on the summit is recorded in Sir William Petty's Atlas of Ireland in 1685, indicating that it survived in some form in spite of oppression. A hermit and pilgrims' guide, Robert Binn (or Bob of the Reek), was present on the summit in the 1830s and is believed to be buried on the site. In 1903 the Archbishop of Tuam re-established the custom of saying Mass on the summit. The last mass held in *Teampall Phádraig*, reputed to be the original structure built by St. Patrick, was on 14th of August 1904, when it was replaced by the modern church, constructed using money raised by subscription. The night pilgrimage was officially discontinued in 1974 but is still undertaken by some hardy souls. It is especially popular with the travelling community who are custodians of many forms of traditional piety.

St. Patrick's Oratory (1905) on the summit of Croagh Patrick.

Archaeological Discoveries on Croagh Patrick

The most significant archaeological discoveries have been the identification of a hillfort and a monastic complex on the summit cone. The hillfort may be the first tangible evidence of a prehistoric presence on the summit. Parallels among other Irish hillforts are difficult to come by. Only the inland promontory fort on the eastern Faha ridge of Mount Brandon is comparable in height (at 2,500ft) and the fort at Caherconree is located on a spur (c.2,000ft). The presence of a hilltop enclosure on Brandon has been suggested but has yet to be confirmed.

The rampart encircling the summit of Croagh Patrick is clearly visible on aerial photographs, together with a score of hut circles outside the rampart. Caesar Otway described a massive cyclopean wall surviving on the north side of the summit in 1839. Part of this stone bank stood until at least 1905 when it was first photographed. It was subsequently flattened during various alterations to the present church. Archaeologists investigated the rampart and hut sites in 1995, recovering glass and amber beads thought to date to the Iron Age, Third Century BC, from the vicinity of the collapsed rampart. Amber and glass beads can also date to the Early Christian Period or later. However, it is possible that the enclosure was related to the monastic remains on the summit rather than predating them.

Other mountain top shrines with ecclesiastical associations include: Slieve League (Co Donegal), Mount Brandon (County Kerry), Slieve Donard (Co Down), Church Mountain (Co Wicklow) and Drung Hill (Co Kerry). The remains of a small church associated with St. Aed Mac Bric have been described in a hollow just below the summit on the eastern side of Slieve League, which also features 26 small cairns that may have been penitential stations. A number of sub-circular house sites have been identified by the author emerging from beneath the eroding peat cover on the west summit that may relate to the use of the mountain in early historic times. They provide a possible parallel for the hut hollows on and around the summit of Croagh Patrick. Mount Brandon and Slieve Donard both have associations with suggested pre-Christian deities.

Wall collapse within the Early Christian Oratory during excavation.

Mount Brandon is particularly significant because the deity in question was Crom Dubh and there was a tradition of a Christian pilgrimage to the site. Two Neolithic cairns on the summit of Slieve Donard (named after St. Donard) may have been utilized as a chapel and a cell respectively in the Christian period. Slieve Donard also had a pilgrimage tradition, which died out in the 18th century. Church Mountain has a church on the summit that has been built on top of a prehistoric cairn that was probably a passage tomb. It also had a pilgrimage tradition and mass was said there once a year until 1798. On the summit of Drung Hill there is a 30m-diameter cairn with a small platform on which there is a cross and ogham inscribed pillar stone. The ogham inscription reads "Maqui R..." (most of it is illegible). The cairn is traditionally the burial place of St. Finian and there was a yearly pilgrimage there on the last Sunday of July, *Domhnach na dTuras*, which ceased in the early twentieth century.

East doorway of Early Christian Oratory during excavation.

Early Christian, 500 - 1000AD

In 1994 a programme of archaeological excavations on the summit of Croagh Patrick focused on a complex of low buildings to the east of the 1905 church, adjacent to *Leaba Phádraig* (St. Patrick's Bed). The work proved spectacularly successful. One of the faint structures turned out to be the lower part of a stone structure. This was interpreted as an upturned boat-shaped oratory (church) similar in design to the famous Gallarus oratory on the Dingle peninsula (Co. Kerry). Initially, doubts were expressed as to whether the structure was an oratory. Its door was in the east wall rather than facing west as is usual. This led to suggestions that it might be a secular building. Rectangular architecture only became popular for secular buildings in Ireland after the period suggested by the radiocarbon dates from Croagh Patrick (see below). Several other oratories are known which do not conform to the usual east-west orientation. Teampall Beanáin overlooking Killeany on the Aran Islands is orientated north-south and an important early hermitage on the inaccessible Bishop's Island off the Clare Coast has its door in the south wall. The unusual orientations of all three seem to be a response to the prevailing wind in highly exposed locations. The oratory on Croagh Patrick is the first tangible evidence of an Early Christian monastic site on the summit and confirms the early references to the existence of a church there.

The oratory, which measures 7.75m x 5.5m externally, with inclined walls and eastern entrance, is one of the earliest dated stone ecclesiastical buildings to be excavated. Fragments of medieval pottery and bronze pins were recovered within the ruins of the oratory. A radiocarbon date of cal. AD 430 – 890 has been returned from charcoal samples taken from within the oratory. The structure is no longer visible as it was carefully backfilled in order to protect it from the long-established practice of taking stones from the mountain as relics.

The dry stone walling of the Early Christian Oratory.

The summit of Croagh Patrick from the East, showing the 1905 Oratory, the Early Christian Oratory and Leaba Phádraig.

Ireland's Holy Mountain

Gallarus Oratory on the Dingle Peninsula, Co. Kerry.

Prehistoric Background

The significance of Croagh Patrick in Early Christian times is emphasized by the presence of at least four ecclesiastical sites on and around the mountain ridge itself. The archaeological evidence discovered thus far supports a Christian presence on the mountain from in or around the sixth century AD, with a possible Iron Age presence dating to eight centuries earlier. It has been suggested, however, that the Croagh Patrick ridge has been utilized as a giant ritual canvas since Neolithic times (4,000BC) and that it was the focus of a prehistoric pilgrimage. The evidence for this is extensive but primarily circumstantial. Nevertheless, the theory has received support from at least one leading scholar and has been used to help interpret at least one other site (Manning, 2002).

The earliest known evidence of human presence in the vicinity of Croagh Patrick dates from the late Mesolithic Period (circa 6000 to 4000 BC). Bann flakes from the shore of Lough Lannagh, near Castlebar and from Burrishoole to the north, are part of a growing body of evidence for an extensive late Mesolithic presence along the coast and river systems throughout western Connacht. These artefacts would have been used by nomadic bands of pre-agricultural hunter-gatherers. The summit would have had an even greater visual signature in the late Mesolithic since it would have been one of the few places above the tree line. Deciduous woodlands blanketed the more gently sloped mountains as well as the lowlands.

More tangible evidence exists for the Neolithic period (4000 – 2000 BC). There are at least two possible megalithic tombs in the vicinity of Croagh Patrick, one to the east and the other to the west. Richard Gillespie has recently excavated a Neolithic house site in the townland of Gortaroe at the edge of Westport. There is also a spectacular Neolithic rock art site at Boheh, on the eastern approach to Croagh Patrick. The Boheh Stone, or "St. Patrick's Chair", is one of the most important rock art sites in Ireland. The other main concentrations of rock art in Ireland are in the southwest in counties Cork and Kerry and in North Donegal.

Killadangan (Annagh) archaeological complex from the north.

It has been theorized that a solar alignment exists between the Boheh stone and the summit of Croagh Patrick. A "rolling sun" phenomenon was first observed by Gerry Bracken, a local scholar. He later published his discovery with Professor P.A. Wayman. From Boheh, the sun appears to sit on the summit of the mountain ridge and then "rolls down" the side of the mountain at sunset. This event takes place on the 18th April (sowing season) and again on the 24th August (the harvest), dates that, along with the Winter Solstice (21st December), divide the year into approximately three parts. The stone was incorporated into the Christian pilgrimage to the summit along the ancient *Tóchar Phádraig* (Patrick's Road Way). This roadway is said to have run for seventy miles from *Rath Croghan*, the royal pagan site of Connacht in the centre of Ireland, westward to the summit. In local folklore it continues onwards to Caher Island in the form of a *Via Sanctorum*, a sub-sea saint's road.

The landscape of Mayo is dotted with evidence of Bronze Age (2000 – 600 BC) activity. Almost all of the visible remains are of a ritual or burial nature, consisting of stone alignments (three or more stones in a row) and groups of standing stones, including a large complex at Killadangan. This site is located on a narrow coastal strip at the northeastern base of the mountain. Approximately 30 *fulachta-fiadha* (Bronze Age cooking sites) were discovered during the course of an archaeological survey and rescue excavations in the Croagh Patrick and Westport area. A number of these were very well preserved with timber troughs and date to the beginnings of the Bronze Age. Some may be related to an equally large number of hut sites on and around the mountain.

The ritual and settlement evidence demonstrate that there was a significant Bronze Age population in the vicinity of Croagh Patrick. This is supported by work on the palaeobotany of the region by NUI Galway. This shows considerable human impact during both the Neolithic and Bronze Ages on the upland landscapes. Bronze Age inhabitants may have been attracted by the mountain's natural resources; the most important being gold and soapstone. At Rosbeg a timber hut-site, excavated by Richard Gillespie and dated to 1200BC, contained a decorated soapstone spindle whorl. A soapstone mould used for making Bronze Axes is known from Culfin on the north Connemara coast a short distance to the southwest.

Inner wall face of rampart surrounding the summit of Croagh Patrick from the south.

Roilig Mhuire (Mary's Graveyard) is a group of three cairns within an irregular enclosure at Carrowmacloughlin and Glencally. These are situated at the base of the cone on the western side and were once believed to be of Bronze Age date. It was believed that they were burial cairns that had been Christianized but John O'Donovan, who visited the site in the mid 19th century, described them as small penitential stations onto which pilgrims deposited stones. The cairns developed over time. They do have a ritual and religious origin but it is one of quite modern date. Another cairn, *Leacht Benain* (named after St. Patrick's charioteer) in the townland of Teevenacroaghy, seems to be a genuine prehistoric antiquity that has been incorporated into the Patrick myth. In recent decades a new cairn of stones, also called *Leacht Benáin,* has been constructed on the main pilgrimage trail, *circa* 30m from the original.

Late Bronze Age/Iron Age (600BC – 400AD) activity in the area may be indicated by the famous Carrowjames Cemetery of ring barrows (circular earthen burial mounds) at Belcarra to the east of Croagh Patrick, by three other ring barrows to the east and southeast, and by a large lake dwelling in Moher Lake to the south. Carrowjames is traditionally considered to date to the Iron Age. Moher Lake Crannog was used by the O'Malleys in the Middle Ages but Late Bronze Age Crannogs are also known and it is almost certain that the O'Malley dwelling was built on top of an earlier structure.

Throughout Ireland there is evidence for a Late Iron Age lull (*circa* 0-300AD) in human activity, which surged again in the Early Christian Period. A sole beehive quern from Boheh and the possible amber beads from the excavations at Croagh Patrick are the sum total of Iron Age material on record, although the ring-barrows and the hill fort on the summit may yet prove to be from this period. The excavation of a ring fort at Lislackagh near Swinford, Co Mayo, revealed three round houses dating to between the 2nd century BC and the 2nd century AD. This exceptionally important site is one of the few dated Iron Age structures in County Mayo. There are a number of other ringforts (raths and cashels) along the lower slopes of the mountain. These indicate a burgeoning Early Christian (500 – 1000AD) population, although in view of the Lislackagh discoveries it is possible that some may date to several centuries earlier.

One of the hut sites on the western slope of Croagh Patrick during excavation.
Mr. Brendan Walsh and Mr. Michael Gibbons

A Ritual Landscape?

It has been argued, most cogently by Christiaan Corlett who has undertaken a great deal of research in the area, that many of the Bronze Age ritual structures were built with the presence of the mountain in mind. Stone alignments, for example, are said to line up on the mountain and individual standing stones are said to be positioned with the summit in view. It is further claimed that the mountain has had a continuing ritual and social significance since at least the late Neolithic and that the landscape of the area was built up in response to the presence of the Holy Mountain. According to this line of reasoning, the incorporation of the mountain into a Christian framework was an acknowledgement by the Christian Church that Croagh Patrick was too powerful a religious symbol to ignore. Crom Dubh or the demonic birds that confronted Patrick are thought to stand in for the old divinities of the mountain. This would fit with the pattern observed in the Classical world and in Britain. The ritual centres of the old order were often converted into Christian cult centres, often with the previous reigning deity serving on under the thin disguise of Christian sanctity.

It must be admitted, however, that the evidence is inconclusive at best. Unlike other mountains such as Slieve Carr (Mayo) or Knocknarea (Sligo) with their Neolithic cairns, there is no evidence of any effort being made to modify the shape of the mountain itself in the Neolithic or Bronze Age. Corlett argues that this was a deliberate policy, to preserve the mountain's sanctity, but there doesn't seem to be any conceivable way to test this. It was once believed that the Boheh stone was the only rock art site in Mayo. This seemed to suggest that it might have been positioned there especially, possibly in view of Croagh Patrick to take advantage of

The summit of Croagh Patrick from the South.

the mountain's sanctity. As Corlett notes, however, it is not the only example of Neolithic rock art in the area. Another was recently discovered at Drumcoggy in the hills overlooking Lough Mask. This example does not seem to have any relationship with Croagh Patrick; in fact the summit is invisible from the site. Its relationship is perhaps with its nearby lake, Loughan na Sí, and St. Patrick's Chair at Boheh also may be positioned with regard to nearby lakes, rather than with the mountain. The "rolling sun" phenomenon is not solely visible from St. Patrick's chair and Van Hoek, a leading expert on rock art, has suggested that the apparent connection between the two may be a coincidence.

Some of the Bronze Age alignments seem to be aligned on prominent features or gaps in the landscape. Many more are not. The overall pattern seems to be of North-South alignment rather than any specific connection to landscape features. Croagh Patrick is indeed visible from many Bronze Age ritual sites, including some at great distances from the mountain, but it is also visible from virtually every modern building in the area. Paradoxically, the dominant visual position of Croagh Patrick across a large area, which makes it a good candidate for a prehistoric ritual centre, also makes it almost impossible to establish whether or not it has any specific connection to any individual site.

Until evidence for some form of prehistoric ritual activity on the summit of the mountain itself becomes available it would be unwise to conclude that pre-Christian activities there prefigured later Christian practices or that there was a pre-Christian pilgrimage to the site. Neither Corlett nor any of the other writers have done so, but, in view of the fact that the theory has begun to influence the interpretation of other mountain sites, it is worth restating that the suggestion, while attractive, remains unproven.

Members of the Croagh Patrick Archaeological Excavation team.
Standing (L-R) Brendan Walsh, Harry Hughes, Chairman, Phelim Gibbons, Michael John Ball, John Cummins,
Front (L-R) Gerry Walsh, Director of Excavations, Michael Gibbons, Director of Survey.

CROAGH PATRICK

A COLLECTION OF AMATEUR AND PROFESSIONAL PHOTOGRAPHS

CAPTURING DECADES OF FACES, MEMORIES AND MYSTICAL

VIEWS OF THE REEK

THESE PHOTGRAPHS WERE SELECTED FROM THE ENTRIES IN THE PHOTOGRAPHY

COMPETITIONS HELD IN 2002 AND 2003

Picture Left: **Reflections of Croagh Patrick** *By Eamonn McCarthy*

Legs and sticks, 1998 *By Chrys Rigavd*

Through the church window *By Córinne Nicholson*

Bina McLoughlin, 'Queen of Connemara', 1986 *By Tom Campbell*

People struggling up and down, 1998 *By Chrys Rigavd*

Bare feet, 1998 *By Chrys Rigavd*

Pilgrims prayer *By Michael O'Sullivan*

Pilgrims progress *By Michael O'Sullivan*

Offerings for oratory *By Michael A. Kelly*

At the statue   *By Michael A. Kelly*

Reflections in the mist *By Tom Campbell*

New Years Day, 2002 *By Michael O'Sullivan*
Second place in the Amateur Section, 2002

Greeting the Pilgrims *By Michael O'Sullivan*
(Archbishop of Tuam, Most Rev. Dr Michael Neary, being greeted by a Pilgrim)

Point of view *By Gianluca Ciralli*

A clear day *By Brian Masterson*

Ireland's Holy Mountain

Keeping an eye on things   *By Rodger Kenny*
(Mr John Cummins and his dog)

A well earned rest *By Eamonn McCarthy*
Fourth place in the Amateur Section, 2002

Cottage Croagh Patrick *By Jerome Hingrat*
Highly Commended, 2002

Waiting for his master *By Rodger Kenny*
(Mr John Cummins on roof)
Highly Commended, 2002

Dressed for the occasion   *By Gerry Campbell*
Highly Commended, 2002

Mum and Dad *By Grainne McCarthy*
First place in the Primary School Section, 2002

Equinox 1 *By Conor McKeown*
Second place in the Professional Section, 2002

Michael Boland and John Callaghan of Co. Sligo *By Michael McLaughlin*
Third place in the Professional Section, 2002

Old Head   *By Ashling McCarthy*
First place in the Secondary School Section and Second place in the Best Overall, 2002

Clouds on the Reek   *By Michael O'Sullivan*

Ireland's Holy Mountain

Aifreann An Blian Nua, 2002 *By Michael O'Sullivan*

Silent Prayer   *By Eamonn McCarthy*

Holy Waters *By Eamonn McCarthy*

"Fancy meeting ewe here" *By Eamonn McCarthy*

Storm on Clew Bay *By Kevin Ryan*

At the foot of Croagh Patrick - Murrisk   *By Margaret Chapman*

Mayo Express   *By Eddie Mallin*

The view *By Eddie Mallin*

Ireland's Holy Mountain

So far so good   *By Eddie Mallin*

The struggle *By Eddie Mallin*

Ireland's Holy Mountain

Prayers in the clouds *By Conor McKeown*

Hurting *By Eddie Mallin*
Second prize in the Amateur Section and Third place Overall, 2003

Ireland's Holy Mountain

Enduring faith   *By Tom Campbell*
First place in the Old Photograph Competition, 2002

Foot massage *By Robert Pipata*

Ireland's Holy Mountain

Prayer *By Robert Pipata*

Souvenirs *By Chrys Rigavd*

Ireland's Holy Mountain

The silhouette of a saint *By Natasha Pincus*

Resting   *By Eamonn McCarthy*
Fourth prize in the Amateur Section, 2003

Hail Good Friday *By Kevin Hoban*

Rosmary Coghlan and her friend Mary of the "Golden Rosary", London *By Michael McLaughlin*

Man of the Reek *By Michael McLaughlin*

Barefoot on the Reek *By Michael McLaughlin*

Ireland's Holy Mountain

On top of the world *By Ursula Staunton*

Taking a breather   *By Irene Fisher*
First prize in the Old Photograph Section, 2003

Ireland's Holy Mountain

Old postcard *Provided by Mary Foley and Des Bourke*

I'm almost there *By Tom Campbell*

Joining in the prayers of the faithful *By Tom Campbell*

Patrick's path *By Ursula Nicholson*

Ireland's Holy Mountain

Mystified *By Des Denny*

Hiking Croagh Patrick *By Samuel Harman Conlon*
Third prize in the Primary School Section, 2003

Wildflowers *By Tiffany Ryce-Kelly*

September *By James Broderick*

In the name of Saint Patrick *By John Corcoran*

The chapel   *By Sonya Taylor*

Pilgrim praying   *By John Corcoran*

Mecca *By Rosario Cooney*

Ireland's Holy Mountain

Resurrection's promise   *By Robert W. Kirkland*

Croagh Patrick - A July twilight *By Michael Mannion*
Highly Commended, 2002

Croagh Patrick *By Davy Walsh*
Highly Commended, 2002

Simply perfect peace *By Síabhra Walsh*
Second place in the Primary School Section, 2002

Ireland's Holy Mountain

A watchful eye *By Natasha Pincus*
Third place in the Amateur Section, 2002

Peaceful, in the shadow of Croagh Patrick *By Sean Burke*
Sixth place in the Amateur Section, 2002

Two monuments *By David Brody*

Sunny Reek *By Vincent Gavin*
Second place in the Secondary School Section, 2002

Penitent pilgrim *By John Corcoran*
First place in the Amateur Section and First place Overall, 2002

Praying the Rosary together *By Tom Campbell*
Third place in the Old Photograph Section, 2002

St. Patrick's bed *By Fr. Brendan McDonagh and entered by Tom O'Malley*
Second place in the Old Photograph Section, 2002

Hot and cold *By Michael McLaughlin*
First place in the Professional Section and Third place Overall, 2002

Still morning *By Mary Dove*

Playing golf *By Theresa Murray*

Ireland's Holy Mountain

Mountain view from Killadangan *By Conor McKeown*

Nestled in the shadow *By Susan Coleman*

Three men in a curragh *By Connie Cullen*

Waiting *By Mara Sola*

Red sky at night *By Liz Kavanagh*

Field of gold *By Liz Kavanagh*

The summit *By Eamonn McCarthy*
First prize in the Amateur Section and First place Overall, 2003

Famine memorial   *By Sarah Ingham*
Fifth place in the Amateur Section, 2002

Solitude *By Liz Kavanagh*

Freedom *By Mara Sola*

Rock of truth *By Mara Sola*

Time is shadowless three *By John Maginness*

Flower opening time - closing time *By John Maginness*

The tough part *By Eddie Mallin*
Fith prize in the Amateur Section, 2003

Descending the scree *By W. McCartney*

"Follow me and you can join me in Heaven someday" *By Áine Cryan*

Ireland's Holy Mountain

Resting on the church steps *By David Brody*
First prize in Secondary School Section, 2003

Contradiction *By Grace Allen*

Purple haze *By Rory O'Malley*

Paddling at sundown *By Rory O'Malley*

Inside St. Patrick's Oratory *By Conor McKeown*

Pilgrims on the summit *By Patrick Reily*

From the beach *By Samuel Harman Conlon*
Second prize in the Primary School Section, 2003

Rock out on the mountain *By David Brody*
Third prize in Secondary School Section, 2003

Sunset over Croagh Patrick *By Gráinne McCarthy*
First prize in Primary School Section, 2003

Frisbee on the beach *By David Brody*
Second prize in Secondary School Section, 2003

Still waters *By Liz Kavanagh*
Sixth prize in the Amateur Section, 2003

Sunset 2001 *By Thomas Sweeney*
Third prize in the Amateur Section, 2003

No living soul *By Derieppe Celine*
Third prize in the Old Photograph Section, 2003

The childrens pilgrimage *By Theresa Murray*
Second prize in the Old Photograph Section, 2003

Evening sail *By Fank Dolan*
Third prize in the Professional Section, 2003

Western light *By Conor McKeown*
Second prize in the Professional Section, 2003

Morning mist *By Fank Dolan*
First prize in the Professional Section and Second place Overall, 2003

Aerial photograph *By Harry Hughes*

Third Station - *Roilig Mhuire* *By Harry Hughes*

Path erosion *By Harry Hughes*

Path and summit circa 1950

Recommended Reading

Bracken, G.G. and Wayman, P.A. (1992) A Neolithic or Bronze Age Alignment for Croagh Patrick, *Cathair na Mart 12*, 1-12

Corlett, Christiaan (1996) Prehistoric Pilgrimage to Croagh Patrick, *Cathair na Mart 16*, 54-61

Corlett, Christiaan (1998) The Prehistoric Ritual Landscape of Croagh Patrick Co. Mayo, *Journal of Irish Archaeology IX*, 9-26

Coyne, Frank and Collins, Tracy (2005) "Mount Brandon Co Kerry – Dingle's Holy Mountain," *Archaeology Ireland: Heritage Guide No.29*

Gibbons, Michael, Higgins, Jim, Gibbons, Myles (2004), "Mapping the Mesolithic in Western Connacht," *IQUA Newsletter* April 2004, 4-7

Gillespie, Richard, Archaeological Excavations on the Westport Main Drainage and Waste Disposal Scheme (2000-2004), *Mayo Co. Council Archaeological Series No.4*   Castlebar (forthcoming)

Hughes, Harry, (1991), *Croagh Patrick (Cruach Phádraig – The Reek): An Ancient Mountain Pilgrimage*, Westport

Manning, Conleth (2002), Church Mountain, Co Wicklow, *Wicklow Archaeology and History Vol 2*, 61-68

Morahan, Leo (ed), 2001 *Croagh Patrick, Co. Mayo: archaeology, landscape and people*, Westport

Ó'Carragáin, Tomás, O'Sullivan, Jerry, Ó'Caoimh, Tomás (2005), "A flying visit to Bishop's Island, Co. Clare, *Archaeology Ireland, Vol 19, No 1, Issue 71*, 34-37

Ó'Cróinín, Dáibhí (2001) "Saint Patrick" in Hughes and Nolan (eds) *Armagh History and Society: Interdisciplinary Essays on the History of an Irish County*, Geography Publications

O'Sullivan and Sheehan (eds) (1996) *The Iveragh Peninsula: An Archaeological Survey of South Kerry,"* Cork

Otway, C., *A Tour in Connaught* comprising sketches of Clonmacnoise, Joyce country and Achill, Dublin (1839)

Van Hoek, M.A.M (1993) *"The Prehistoric rock art of the Boheh Stone, Co. Mayo,"* Cathair na Mart 13, 1-15

Walsh, Gerry (1994) *"Preliminary Report on the Archaeological Excavations on the Summit of Croagh Patrick,"* Cathair na Mart 14, 1-11

Croagh Patrick Publications

Croagh Patrick - An Ancient Mountain Pilgrimage by Harry Hughes (1991)

Croagh Patrick - Ireland's Holy Mountain - Brochures available in English, French and German (1997)

Croagh Patrick - Archaeology, Landscape and People by Leo Morahan (2001)

Tóchar Phádraig - A Pilgrim's Progress Ballintubber to Croagh Patrick (1989)

Clew Bay Archaeological Trail by Edel Hackett (2003)

Websites www.croaghpatrick.org and www.clewbaytrail.com

Aerial photograph *By Harry Hughes*